TRY IT !

How Frieda Caplan
Changed the Way We Eat

written by
Mara Rockliff

illustrated by
Giselle Potter

Beach Lane Books
New York London Toronto Sydney New Delhi

When Frieda Caplan went to work at the Seventh Street produce market, she saw boxes of bananas.

Piles of potatoes.

Truckloads of tomatoes.

Apples as far as the eye could see.

Buyers came to order fruits and vegetables for restaurants, grocery stores, and roadside stands. *Everyone* ate apples and bananas and potatoes and tomatoes. So the market sold a *lot*.

Now, there was nothing wrong with a potato. Still, Frieda thought, why not give something new a try?

"What about these nice fresh mushrooms?" Frieda asked.

The men at the market told her, "Nobody eats those."

Frieda thought more people might eat mushrooms if they had the chance.

Try it!

Frieda was persistent.
She liked selling mushrooms.
And people started to like eating them.

They ordered them at restaurants.

They tossed them in their
carts at the grocery store.

They snatched them up at roadside stands.

Soon, Frieda had her own spot at the market.
While the men went on selling apples and bananas
and potatoes and tomatoes, she sold mushrooms—
and more.

Go See Frieda.

Frieda got a funny feeling in her elbows when she tasted something
new and special, something she was sure people would like to try.

With a good name . . .

We call them
Chinese gooseberries!

But they come from
New Zealand!

Well, they are brown
and fuzzy like a
kiwi bird....

PRODUCT OF
New Zeala

a sticker to explain what was inside . . .

and maybe a recipe or two . . .

who wouldn't want to taste something
a little different from an ordinary apple or potato?

Especially if it was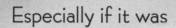

CRISPY...

Jicama

CRUNCHY...

Sugar Snap pea

JUICY...

blood Orange

CREAMY...

cherimoya

SWEET...

champagne grape

Asian pear

OR SPICY!

black radish

It took a while for everybody to get used to Frieda's funny-looking fruits.

"A watermelon can't be seedless!"

seedless watermelon, 1962

But if Frieda felt it in her elbows,
she knew it was going to catch on . . .
eventually.

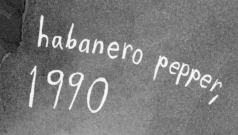

habanero pepper,
1990

dragon fruit,
1994

Buddha's
hand,
2000

mangosteen,
2008

fresh lychee,
2015

The Seventh Street produce
market still had boxes of bananas,
piles of potatoes, truckloads of
tomatoes, and apples as far as the eye
could see. But now, thanks to Frieda,
it also had mounds of mangosteen,
heaps of jicama, and quantities of quince.

Year after year, Frieda kept coming up with fresh ideas— and everybody was all ears. (Especially about the baby corn!)

Farmers dug for tips on what to grow.

How about purple potatoes?

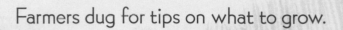

Cooks peppered her with questions.

Reporters pleaded for a scoop about the next big thing.

It might be prickly . . .

nopale
(cactus pad)

gooey . . .

passion fruit

funny-shaped . . .

star fruit

or flat.

Donut Peach

If Frieda felt it in her elbows, that was that.

Of course, even Frieda didn't like *everything*.
But she was always willing to try.

durian

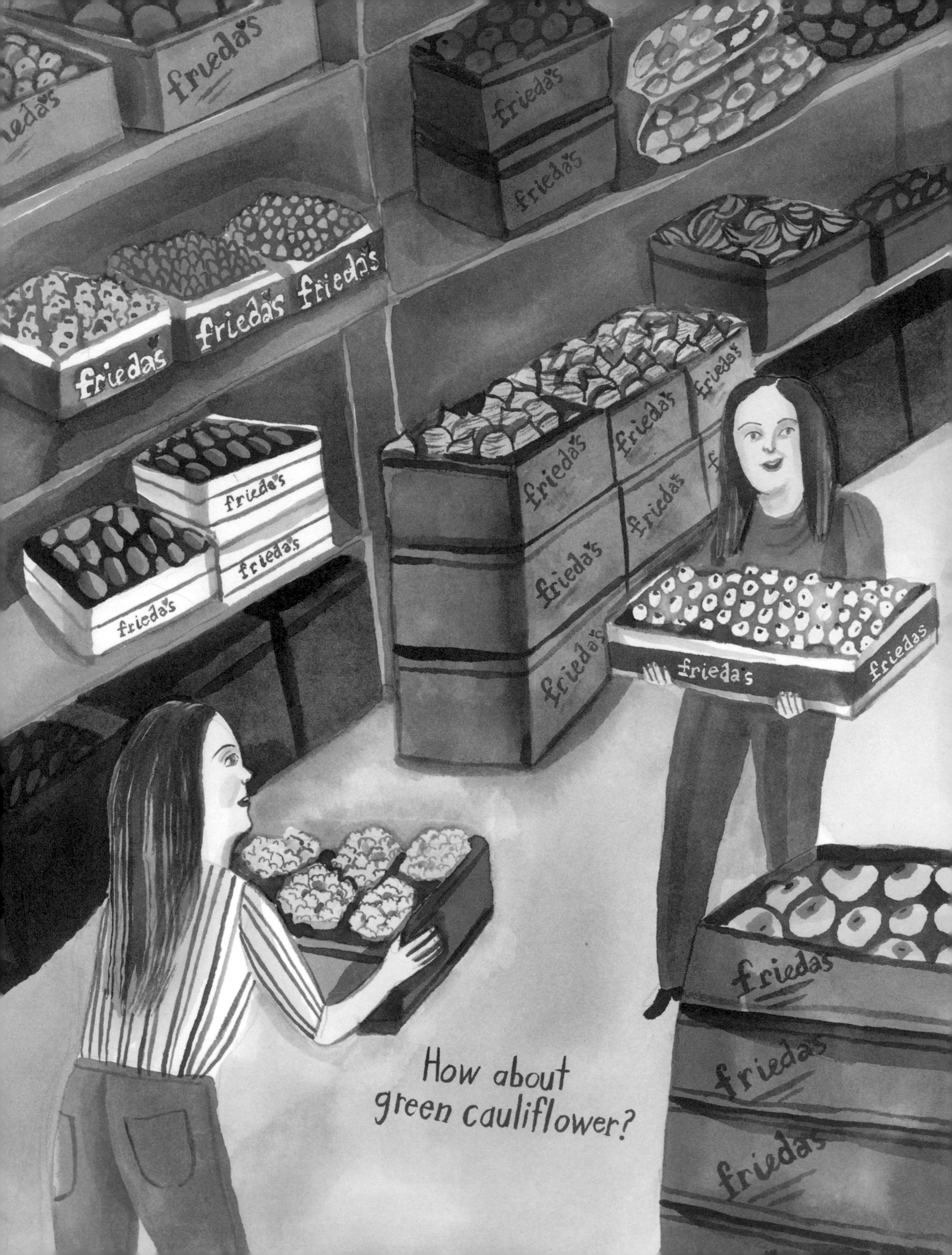

How about
green cauliflower?

Frieda's grown-up daughters came to work with her, and they had fresh ideas, too.

Why not yellow tomatoes?

Or purple asparagus?

frieda's

frieda's

frieda's

DON'T FEAR THE FRUIT—
Even if it looks weird, really weird!

Dragon fruit

HOTTEST CHILI PEP
IN THE WORLD!

Together, they found even more surprising fruits and vegetables to put in supermarkets and on dinner tables all across America.

Because once people have eaten apples and bananas,
purple potatoes and yellow tomatoes,
kiwifruit and sugar snap peas and spaghetti squash . . .

who knows *what* they'll try next?

Fabulous, Fearless ... Frieda!

Have you ever tasted kiwifruit? Did you know watermelon can be yellow inside? When you walk into a supermarket, can you spot any fruits or vegetables you've never tried? If your answer is yes, thank Frieda Caplan, produce pioneer.

Frieda Rapoport Caplan was born in 1923 in Los Angeles, California. Her parents were Russian Jewish immigrants who taught her to work hard and keep an open mind.

In 1956, as a new mother, Frieda took a job as a bookkeeper at the Seventh Street produce market in Los Angeles. Soon after, she moved into sales. All the other salespeople were men, but that didn't stop Frieda. She loved people. She loved to talk. And it turned out she had a knack for talking people into trying something new.

Frieda started her own produce company in 1962. Every morning, she popped out of bed at 2:00 a.m., put on lipstick and high heels, and drove to the market, where she caught buyers' attention with her unusual produce and her purple signs.

Frieda was the first woman in the United States to own and operate a wholesale produce business, but putting baby carrots and spaghetti squash in supermarkets wasn't the only way she changed people's minds. In 1979, when Frieda was honored as "Produce *Man* of the Year," she handed the award right back. Soon after, the award was given a new name: Produce Marketer of the Year.

Of all the fruits and vegetables Frieda made popular, the most famous was the kiwifruit. Over the years, Frieda tasted so many, she developed an allergy to kiwi! Luckily, she could still eat her very favorite edible plant, the funny-looking artichoke—as long as someone else prepared it for her. Frieda never learned to cook.

Frieda's two daughters, Karen and Jackie, grew up working at their mother's company during summers and after school. Today, they own Frieda's Inc. Two granddaughters, Alex and Sophia, also joined the family business before Frieda died in 2020 at the age of ninety-six. She enjoyed a long and *fruitful* life.

When Frieda started selling produce, the average supermarket carried about sixty-five kinds of fruits and vegetables. Now shoppers can find seven to eight hundred, many of them introduced by Frieda's. But Frieda Caplan did much more than sell Americans on tomatillos and alfalfa sprouts, or even mangosteen and quince. She taught us that tasting unfamiliar foods could be a fun adventure—and delicious, too.

A scientist once told Frieda that there are up to eighty thousand edible species of plants on Earth. Frieda was ready to try them all.

Are you?

Frieda

Karen

Jackie

Alex

A Note on Sources

Try It! was based primarily on the many articles about Frieda Caplan published in newspapers and magazines between 1961 and 2020. Among the most informative were "Strange Fruits" by Erik Larson (*Inc.* magazine, November 1989); "Mother Gooseberry" by John Merryman (*Orange Coast Magazine*, March 1995); "Peeling Away the Mystery" by Marlene Parrish (*Pittsburgh Post-Gazette*, June 29, 1997), and "How This Produce Pioneer Popularized the Kiwi and Forever Changed the American Palate" by Kim Lachance Shandrow (Entrepreneur.com, July 16, 2015). Also helpful was the excellent 2015 documentary film about Frieda, *Fear No Fruit*, directed by Mark Brian Smith.

Special thanks to Karen Caplan (Frieda's daughter and the president and CEO of Frieda's Inc.), who patiently answered many questions and reviewed the manuscript for accuracy. Thanks as well to Cindy Sherman and others at Frieda's Inc. who provided information, historical photos, and encouragement.

To Lillian Bird, to make your reading life *even better*. And to the
wonderful people of PJ Library and the Harold Grinspoon Foundation,
for inspiring me to find out what Jewish women have done.—M. R.

For Pia, who loves to try new food,
and Izzy, who doesn't . . . yet!—G. P.

BEACH LANE BOOKS • An imprint of Simon & Schuster
Children's Publishing Division • 1230 Avenue of the Americas,
New York, New York 10020 • Text copyright © 2021 by
Mara Rockliff • Illustrations copyright © 2021 by Giselle
Potter • All rights reserved, including the right of reproduction
in whole or in part in any form.

BEACH LANE BOOKS is a trademark of
Simon & Schuster, Inc. • For information about special
discounts for bulk purchases, please contact Simon &
Schuster Special Sales at 1-866-506-1949
or business@simonandschuster.com.

The Simon & Schuster Speakers
Bureau can bring authors to
your live event.

For more information or to
book an event, contact the
Simon & Schuster Speakers
Bureau at 1-866-248-3049
or visit our website at
www.simonspeakers.com.

Book design by Lauren Rille
The text for this book was set in
Bernhard Gothic. • The illustrations
for this book were rendered
in watercolor.
Manufactured in China • 1020 SCP
First Edition
10 9 8 7 6 5 4 3 2 1

CIP data for this book is available from the
Library of Congress.
ISBN 978-1-5344-6007-2
ISBN 978-1-5344-6008-9 (eBook)